The Ultimate Stand

❖ ❖ ❖

Poetry for the deer hunter

Please refer to the inside back cover
for ordering information

The Ultimate Stand

Poetic Tales of Deer Hunting from the Pearly Swamp Camp

Original Poetry and Illustrations by Mert Cowley

Banksiana Publishing / Chetek, WI

Copyright © 1990 by Mert Cowley/Banksiana Publishing Co..

Illustrations copyright © 1990 by Mert Cowley/Banksiana Publishing Co.

All rights reserved. Except for use in a review, the reproduction or utilization of any of this work in any form or by electronic, mechanical, or other means, now known or hereafter invented, including xerography, photo copying, and recording, and in any information storage and retrieval system is forbidden without the expressed written permission of the publisher.

All correspondence and inquiries
should be directed to
Banksiana Publishing Company
611 22-3/4 Street
Box 804
Chetek, WI 54728

Manufactured in the United States of America.

Main entry under title: The Ultimate Stand.
Summary: A collection of poetry directed towards the deer hunter.

Library of Congress Catalog Card Number 90-84001

ISBN 0-9627867-0-5

FIRST EDITION
10 9 8 7 6 5 4 3 2

1345/2000

Dedication

Sincere thanks to:

my dad—	for introducing me to deer hunting so many years ago
my wife Kathy—	for her patience, love and understanding
my sons Dan and Dave—	for keeping the hunt alive for me
my grandson Joey—	may he inherit my love for the outdoors
my good friend Bill Rhiger—	who helped build the Pearly Swamp Camp and make a dream come true
my fellow teacher Bev Peterson—	for her constructive criticisms and constant urging to put this book together
my friend Dick Kaner—	whose deer hunting enthusiasm is contagious
my campmates—	Myron, Scott, and Kirk, members of the Pearly Swamp Camp
and ALL my fellow hunters—	for their devotion to and admiration of the whitetail deer.

Foreword

If successful deer hunting was accomplished only by skillful hunters after a long and resourceful stalk, this book would be pure nonsense.

But deer hunting involves all of us, the young, the old, the seasoned veteran, and the rank amateur. It includes those who rely on skill, and those whose only chance is predicated by just plain luck. Deer hunting is not only an adventure, but misadventure.

Deer hunting, when distilled to it essence, is memories ... of impossible shots and incredulous misses ... of dreams and of nightmares ... of camp and of camp life ... and of ghostly brown bucks. It's fogged scopes, misfires, and frozen actions. It's snow and rain, bone chilling cold, teeth chattering, and frozen fingers and feet. In the slashings, the swamps, and the jackpines, with rifle, bow and muzzle loader, Mert Cowley has been there. This teacher and poet has been on stand to watch the dawn break. He knows the feelings and expectations, the success and the disappointment.

Deer hunting. Mert Cowley has been there. Thank goodness he was.

Dick Kaner
WJMC Radio AM/FM
Rice Lake, WI

Preface

Several books are available which inform the deer hunter HOW to hunt. Few books have been written advising these same hunters HOW NOT to hunt.

I saw a need to describe hunts that no deer hunter in their right mind would want to remember, and to introduce these hunters to campmates they would never want to share a bunk with.

—Mert Cowley

Table of Contents

Welcome xi
The Shack 1

Some of the Neighbors

Deer Camps—Past and Present
    Near and Far 9

Some of the Gang

Weak-Eyes Sweeny 15
Buck Fever Malone 20
Bear Breath Calhoun 24
Norm and Arlo's Secret 30
Lester's Wardrobe 37
The Monster Recreated 44
The Revenge of Ralph
    The Camp Cook 52
Whitetail Barney's Buddy 59

Life's Little Necessities

The Forkhorn Insurance Agency 66
The Sportsman's License 68
Sound Advice 72
The Prayer 73
Harsh Realities of Camp Life 74

Some of the Hunts
- The Ultimate Stand 78
- Willie and the Aerial Drive 89
- The Dream 99

The Serious Side
- The Bog 103
- The Rub 117
- The Scrape 122
- The Passing of My Pardner—
  The End of an Era 126
- Advice from Dad 128

Closin' Up the Camp
- Camp Scenes—
  Some of the Memories 129
- From the Camp Log 135
- Closing Words 141

Welcome to the Pearly Swamp Camp

We've been waiting for you.

Glad you could make it.

The Shack

Tar paper held by rows of lath
    with musty smells within
The Jackpine Castle may be built
    of log or rusty tin
The roof may leak, the porch may sag
    its curtains held by tack
When season is approaching
    you'll be "heading for The Shack."

"The Crex Meadow Camp"
Burnett Co., WI

THE SHACK

The Shack may be a
    Place for you
to just kick up
    your heels

THE SHACK

A place to come
    and warm yourself
to have a hearty meal

THE SHACK

A deck of cards
    and five card draw
or rest your weary bones

Friends to share
  your hunt with
and never feel alone

To take your turn
    to stoke the stove
and dry your
    soggy boots

THE SHACK

To clean and wipe
 the barrel
of the gun you
 seldom shoot

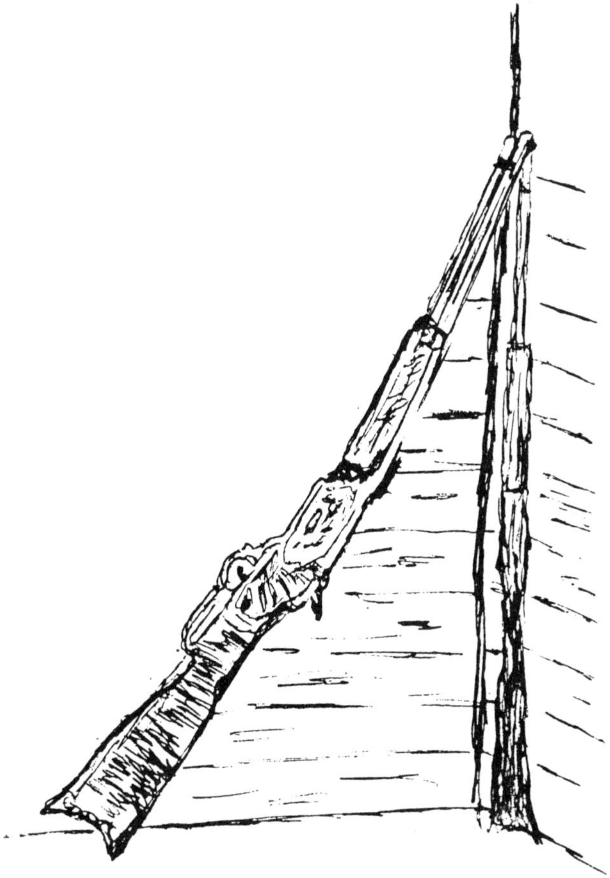

And at the end of season
    when you're closin' up The Shack
You know you're always welcome
    whenever you come back.

Some of The Neighbors Past and Present Near and Far

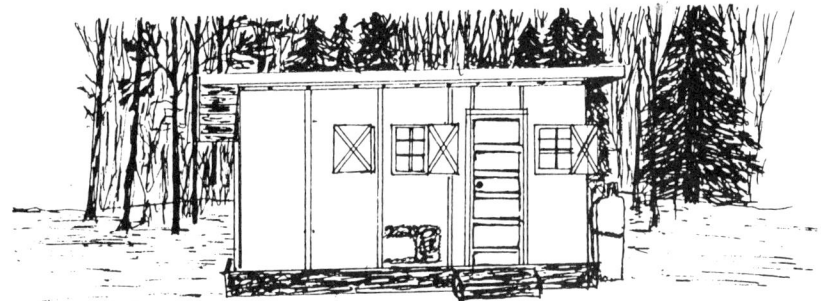

Pearly Swamp Camp #1 • Burnett Co., WI

Pearly Swamp Camp #2 • Burnett Co., WI

"Old Bullet" The Mobile Camp

"Gut Shot Knob"
Burnett Co., WI

Smith Lake Camp
Twn. of Barnes
Bayfield Co., WI

Nehr-Bit Lodge
Burnett Co., WI

The "Stuckert Camp"
Highway 35
Burnett Co., WI

Tim's Place
Highway 35
Burnett Co., WI

Reuilles Retreat
Douglas Co., WI

The "Hilton"
Douglas Co., WI

Buck's Lodge • Axehandle Lake
Chippewa Co., WI

Tyson's Shack
Douglas Co., WI

Dick & Jodie's Place
Brule, WI

"The Camp"
Washburn Co., WI

"The Shack"
Marathon Co., WI

Thompson Camp
Weyerhauser Land
Bayfield Co., WI

Camp St. Croix
Burnett Co., WI

Highway 35 • South of Cozy Corners
Douglas Co., WI

Some of the Gang

Weak-Eyes Sweeny 15

Buck Fever Malone 20

Bear Breath Calhoun 24

Norm and Arlos's Secret 30

Lesters Wardrobe 37

The Monster Recreated 44

The Revenge of
    Ralph The Camp Cook 52

Whitetail Barney's Buddy 59

Weak-Eyes Sweeny

Weak-Eyes Sweeny took a bead,
At what he thought a buck indeed.
With horns like branches on its head,
With careful aim he dropped it dead.

It never moved from where it stood,
He ambled over thinking he would gut the thing
And drag it back and brag aloud that such a rack
Had never hung from off the pole
Since camp had started long ago.

Weak-Eyes knelt beside his kill
Admired it as hunters will.
A stately trophy, truly regal
He'd keep this one strictly legal.
With all his strength, and all his might,
He attached his tag, and locked it tight.

He realized the drag was long.
But knew his compass wasn't wrong.
He took a reading, grabbed the rope,
And started up the awful slope.

Two hours passed before the crest.
And at the top he paused to rest.
Thoughts of camp, a good warm meal
And after supper, cards to deal.

A million thoughts went through his mind.
A-hah he laughed, the buck pool's mine!
For all the years, I've entered it,
I've never won, but didn't quit.

WEAK-EYES SWEENY

His strength returned, he took the rope,
And worked his prize back down the slope.
The big spruce swamp then blocked his trail,
But he pulled and struggled and didn't fail.

He hit the tote road, tired and damp
A mile more he'd be in camp.
A shortcut crossing Rocky Crick,
Would get him back just twice as quick.

T'was way past dark when he hit the drive,
He called, "Come out," and the camp came alive.
In long johns and red shirts, all sorts of attire,
On the porch they all gathered, Sweeny's buck to admire.

Weak-Eyes then said, "Boys, I've something to say,
That nickname you gave me has caused me dismay-
For twenty odd years. I've not said one word."
But for awe of his trophy his speech went unheard.

Then Big Ralph, the camp cook, stepped out of the crowd.
His voice trembled a little as he tried to speak loud,
"That nickname we call you isn't meant to be mean
We like you in camp, if the truth could be seen.

We got real worried when you didn't show,
But we didn't know which way to look or to go.
Weak-Eyes we've called you, for fear of being shot,
So we made a decision, here's what we've got.

We took a collection, charged each one a fee,
And bought you some glasses, so now you can see.
Put them on, turn around, you old swamp buck's rump
That deer that you dragged in,
is an old Pine tree stump."

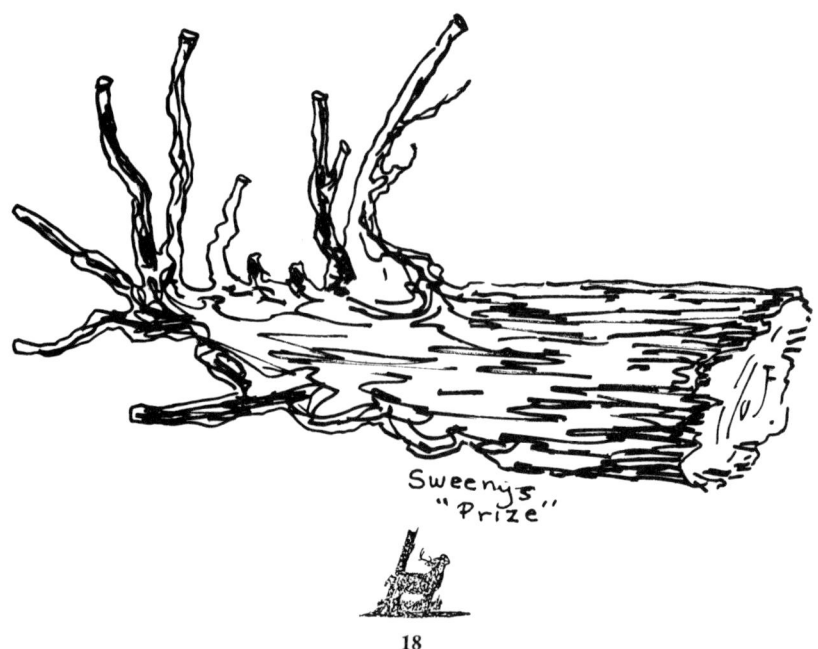

Sweeny's "Prize"

WEAK-EYES SWEENY

Back home,

Sweeny tells it like it was.

Buckfever Malone

Buckfever Hisself

Perhaps it's not fair, now our campmate is gone
To tell all the world of the things he did wrong
But somehow I feel that the tale should be known
The camplife misfortunes, of Buckfever Malone

His nickname he earned, his first day in our camp
When his gun wouldn't fire, cause the action was damp
The mud in his Marlin was stuck like a tick
He fell off a beaver dam, when he tripped on a stick

He went back to camp, hung his clothes up to dry
And planned where he'd go, for the next place to try
Thinking that swamps weren't the places to be
He hit for the oaks, and put his stand up a tree

The men still in camp, as they're sitting around
Still shudder with fear, and their hearts start to pound
As their minds do recall a blood curdling sound
Malone's thirty-foot scream as he fell to the ground

Well somehow Malone didn't die from his fall
He shook himself off, and then stood real tall
And said, "Boys, it's great just being alive,
Let's gather the gang, and then go on a drive"

The group was assembled, assignments were made
Who would walk, who would stand, oh, the best plans were laid
And Malone on his stand, bucks missed numbered five
Exhausted, the drivers said, "Malone screwed up the drive"

SOME OF THE GANG

Dejected, crestfallen, a misfit was he
Malone quit as a hunter, for the camp cook to be
His first evening meal, dressing garnished with berries
Caused us nearly to die, from the camp dysentery

Malone crawled in his bunk, for some time just to think
And three hours later something started to stink
Malone fell asleep with a smoke in his hand
Burned his bunk, a down pillow, and as old bedside stand

Alone the next morning, as he peered through the snow
Out the back door there stood a huge buck and a doe
He shot from the kitchen, three curtains did scorch
Shot the door from the hinges, and collapsed the back porch

He jumped in his pickup, to just take a cruise
The way things were going, he had nothing to lose
Not safe on the road, in the woods, or at camp
He proceeded to drive off a boat landing ramp

BUCK FEVER MALONE

He adjourned to a tavern to help drown his sorrow
In hopes that his luck would be better tomorrow
Feeling much better, he stood up to leave,
Sprained both of his ankles, dislocated his knee

Malone had his bags packed, when we came from our stands
He said, "Boys, I'm dangerous with a gun in my hands
I'm not mad, but I'm leaving, it's obvious to see
That deer hunting and camplife is just not for me

Thanks a lot fellas, but I'm heading home"
Were the last words in camp ever spoke by Malone
Had Malone ever come back, we're all firm believers
He'd a died in the woods, from a case of Buck Fever

SOME OF THE GANG

Bear Breath Calhoun

Deer camps in general, one usually can find
That one of its members stands out in your mind
Such is the case, for he stood all alone
Was the campmate we nicknamed, Bear Breath Calhoun.

Calhoun seemed quite normal, when he joined our group
And probably still would be if not for the soup
That Big Ralph, the camp cook, made on the stove
And was planning to flavor, with a big garlic clove.

It seems that Calhoun, who had nothing to do
Strolled into the kitchen for something to chew
Spotting the garlic clove, he took a bite
Then devoured the whole thing in utter delight.

Not to offend him, we offered a mint
Then Ralph called him "Bear Breath" so that he'd take a hint
But Calhoun kept on eating, till we all hit the rack
And by morning had downed, the whole five-pound sack.

With the sound of the frying pans, we slowly arose
To the strong smell of garlic that dwelled in our nose
Then Whitetail Barney screamed, "Oh, I suppose
The smell of that garlic's all over my clothes."

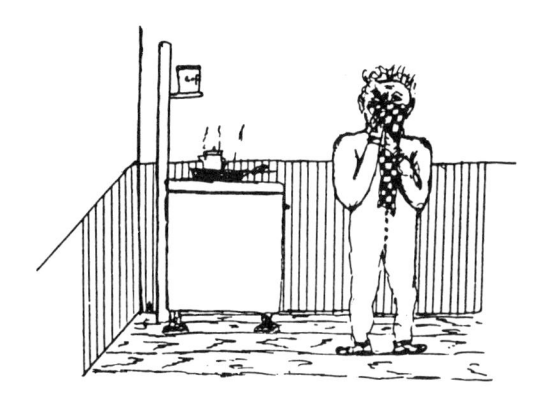

Well, we gathered for breakfast, and all took our seat
For a breakfast of pancakes and bacon to eat
When Bear Breath said, "Morning," my fork hit the rug
And the pure maple syrup, oozed back *into* the jug.

None of us finished our now-tainted meal
And just to stand up, was a painful ordeal
We hit for our stands, by the light of the moon
Told Bear Breath we *might* see him, somewhere around noon.

SOME OF THE GANG

Calhoun entered the woods, and he walked with the wind
About half past eight, I caught scent of him
Tears came to my eyes, and my sinus did run
I had a shortness of breath, till I thought I was done.

But something amazing transpired that day
It's still talked of in camp, even today
For "Bear Breath" became the only man that's alive
Who can walk in a woods, and make a one-man drive.

The deer fled their woodland, by leaps and by bounds
Utter chaos resulted with terrible sounds
Behind laid the forest in a sad state of ruin
Caused by a sneeze, from out of Calhoun.

But we let the deer by, we believe in fair chase
We could have just as well left, our guns in their case
It just makes us sick, we completely despise
To take shots at a deer, that has tears in its eyes.

Things got even worse after supper that night
At our game of five card 'neath the dim corner light
Ralph held a full house, so the story is told
But when Bear Breath said "Paaass" even Ralph had to fold.

Ole and Lena jokes, couldn't be told
We shuddered with fear, there were none that were bold
'nough to till jokes like we did in the past
For fear that Bear Breath might burst forth with a laugh.

SOME OF THE GANG

We were no longer welcome, at the local saloon
'cause of one thoughtless belch from our campmate Calhoun
The bartender screamed, "It's a sneak gas attack"
And forty-four patrons, fled out the back.

When things settled down, and they filed back in,
They all said, "Get out", expecially *HIM*
When Bear Breath said, "Bye," the bouncer did swoon
And the old nickelodeon, played out of tune.

We went back to camp, and just moped around
Lost in our thoughts as we paced up and down
Who thought of it first, no one can say
But Calhoun on his stand, wasn't bothered by jays.

The red squirrels and chickadees had left him alone
Bear Breath could just concentrate on deer sounds alone
And Bear Breath was first, back in camp with his buck
Perhaps the garlic, was part of his luck!

Then and there we decided, we all voted, "Aye"
Not to worry so much of what others would say
We eat garlic for breakfast, along with Calhoun
And our buck pole is filled, usually by noon.

Norm and Arlo's Secret

Ralph's sudden statement caught the whole gang off guard
For brilliant ideas in camp, come by hard.
"We really should know, where the others will be,
In case of a storm or severe injury."

"You're right," chimed in Barney, "it just makes good sense,
When we deer hunt in country so vast and immense
Should one of us get hurt, or can't find our way,
The others should know where to look on that day."

Smokepole then spoke up, suggesting, "Perhaps,
We can solve such a problem with a detailed map.
We'll put it right here, tack it up on the wall;
Then each mark his stands so they're well-known to all."

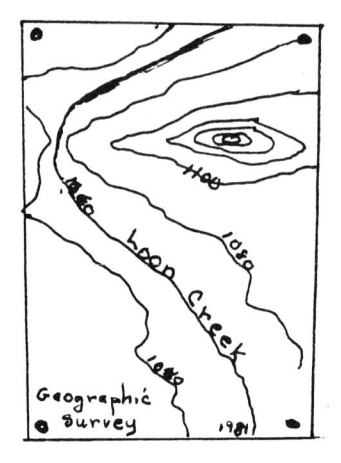

Weak-eyes declared, "This will be a real snap,"
As he unrolled his new Geological Map.
"We'll attach our stand's name, with a large common pin.
And the places we hunt, we can just color in."

Ralph spoke up first, "Mine is named Triple Oaks."
"Mine's The Old Popple," Weak-eyes then spoke.
"Mine's The Big Rock," added Calhoun.
"And mine's the Skunks Den," Barney then swooned.

The two oldest hunters left in our bunch
Had both gone to sleep right after our lunch.
Norman and Arlo had both tuned us out
As both had expired on the old foldout couch.

"Wake up," Barney shouted, in hopes they would hear.
"Did you come up to camp, to sleep or hunt deer?
We need your stand's name, to complete our new map.
Just give the location and return to your nap."

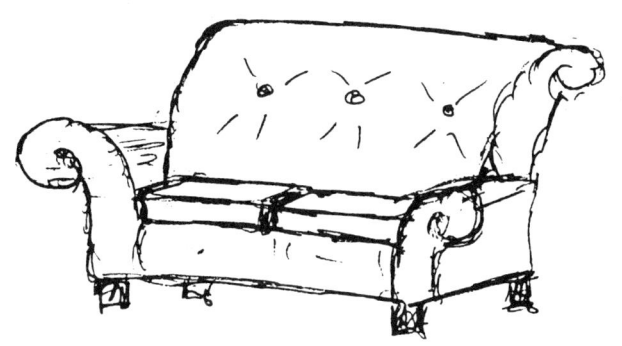

SOME OF THE GANG

Of the two, Norm was first to answer us back.
"For years I have called my best stand "The Rack".
But I've kept it a secret; its location is best
If others should find it, I just couldn't rest."

"Me, too," Arlo said, "if I told you, you'd laugh,
You'd be at my stand till you'd beaten a path.
For the site of my stand is a well-known location
So I just call my deer stand, The Old Excavation."

With that they both drifted back into their sleep
The site of their stands was a secret they'd keep.
We looked at each other and just shook our heads,
Then we finished our map, and we all hit for bed.

NORM AND ARLO'S SECRET

As the rays of the sun found their way through the pines,
On stand, all the hunters had bucks on their minds.
That is except Norm as he drove down the road,
And Arlo who sat, with his gun yet to load.

Norm made a U-turn and was now heading back
When his truck found the ditch, a half mile from the shack.
Knowing he'd never remove it alone
Grabbed his thermos, and rifle and headed for home.

Approaching the driveway, strange sounds did he hear.
The faint sound of music now entered his ear.
To pinpoint the source where sounds would be made
He fine tuned and turned up, his old hearing aid.

The source located with slow noiseless stalk
Norm then made his way down the cold snow-packed walk
To the two-holer house, all boxed up with tin.
He then kicked the door of the outhouse in.

Norm wished at first he weren't there alone.
Had some woods spirit made this place its home?
Fearing the worst, but as big as you'd please
Sat Arlo, his rifle, across his knees.

"Arlo Smith, you should be ashamed,
I can see why you gave your stand its name.
While we hunt all the swamps with frozen feet
You set in here on a padded seat."

"On top of that you complain of cold
And then say it's cause you're getting old.
But you sit all day, you little cheater,
Right next to a large catalytic heater."

Then Arlo, his composure gained,
Said, "Norm, your voice sounds terribly strained.
You sound to me like you're really mad
But deep inside you should be glad.

I knew you'd catch me within time
But you surprised me coming in at nine.
For years you've stayed out until ten
Before you'd come to camp again.

I've watched for years, as you'd come back
Set your alarm, crawl in "The Rack"
Awake by three, and leave again
Then at closing time, you'd come back in.

I then had to listen as you told your lies
About all the big bucks you have surprised.
They all have escaped, or so it would seem
But I know you saw them in your dreams.

SOME OF THE GANG

For years now your secret I have kept,
I remember once, Norm, how you overslept.
T'was I who awoke you by shaking "The Rack"
Or you'd have been caught, when the others came back.

When we built up this camp, it was then all agreed
That we'd hunt as we wished, come and go as we pleased.
And for sixty some seasons we gave it our all
But lately the years started taking their toll.

But we no longer have to hang up a deer
As we once thought we had to, to have a good year.
For fun and enjoyment we've sure had our share
It's now for our sons and their kids that we care.

We both know the problem though we'd never admit
That we're old but too stubborn and ornery to quit.
We perish the thought that we might have to say
We can't stand the cold, and still hunt the whole day."

One of them winked; both started to grin
They knew if they fought, that neither would win
On a handshake, a pact made, the reasons are clear
Now the two just trade stands, every other year.

Lester's Wardrobe

As Lester turned the pages of his regulation book
Before him there in bold print
      was a law he'd overlooked.
The new law stated clearly,
      "No hunter may wear red,"
This season, for the first time,
      "They must wear orange instead."

The shock of such a drastic change
      caught Lester unprepared,
"How can they just pass laws like this
      with no tradition spared?
To hunt for deer in coats of red,
      is 'Mother's Apple Pie'.
You don't just change a good thing
      if there's no darn reason why."

Complaints he made then to his wife
      just fell upon deaf ear.
"Those wore out hunting clothes you have,
      I look at every year."
I just say "Good. I think it's time, I'll tell you
      what I'd do
Get rid of all that old stuff, and start out completely new."

SOME OF THE GANG

So Lester took his box of gear, and
    spread it on the floor,
Each item held a memory
    of many hunts before.
His coat, his shirt, and hunting cap
    of wool were worn thin,
All red and black of checkered weave
    had helped him blend right in.

He fondly held his Guide Boots that he'd
    bought from L.L. Bean,
The finest pair of hunting boots
    that Lester'd ever seen.
His hunting coat from Munsingwear
    he'd used for twenty years,
His lucky pair of old Malones
    had stood by many deer.

By now a tiny tear had formed
    in the corner of his eye,
He sadly shrugged his shoulders
    as inside he wondered, "Why?"
He gently took his hunting gear
    and placed it in a sack,
Then dropped it off at Goodwill,
    and he never once looked back.

LESTER'S WARDROBE

With list in hand he drove straight to
    the local shopping mart,
Grabbed all the sale bills he could
    and giant shopping cart.
Then Lester stood in total awe
    right there in aisle four,
"How can so many things of orange
    be found in just one store?"

He marveled in astonishment,
    "Deer must be found in places,
Many thousand miles away-
    pursued by many races!"
"There's items here from far Japan, Hong Kong and even France,
    And hunting gear made in Taiwan
The bucks wouldn't have a chance."

He grabbed a shirt, some socks and pants
    and a bright orange hunting cap,
Complete with furry ear flaps and
    adjustable chin strap.
Into his cart went one of each
    adding to his hoard,
It reminded him of Sunday noon
    at the local smorgasbord.

Lester's cart was piled high
    he checked his shopping list,
Made certain there was nothing else
    he needed or he'd missed.
At home he took the tags off
    and he packed his hunting box
Complete with extra long johns and three extra pairs of socks.

SOME OF THE GANG

Lester on his stand at dawn
    made quite a brilliant dude,
Who normally excited,
    sat in a pensive mood.
His pals had called him "Manderine"
    as he had left the shack,
Then Lester thought, "I'll show them,
    when I bring a big buck back."

A sloppy snow the night before
    had turned now to a mist,
As miserable an opener as
    one could ever guess.
The breeze that blew at six o' clock
    had turned now to a wind,
Became a hunter's nightmare as
    the snow came in again.

As Lester peered across the slope
    he noticed something wrong
T'was getting dark instead of light
    with the near approach of dawn.
An inner fear "Has blindness struck
    and chosen me at will?"
Then realized his cap was soaked
    and just collapsed the bill.

A glance down toward his brand new gloves
    with trigger finger slits,
"That's funny. When I bought these things
    they really seemed to fit."
The thread they'd used to sew the gloves
    it simply wasn't there,
Instead of just his trigger finger,
    all ten were hanging bare.

His size 9 pair of snowboots which
    were shipped in from Taiwan,
Had soaked more water in them than
    you'd need to float a swan.
Les drained the water from them and
    then tried to wring the felt,
His foot looked like a muskrat with a water-soaked old pelt.

The snows that fell upon the stump
    where Lester chose to set,
Had melted ever slowly, got his seat
    completely wet.
The region of his dampness had a sudden
    nervous twitch,
That turned into a gnawing, painful,
    agonizing itch.

SOME OF THE GANG

Lester scrambled for the brush
    much quicker than a flash,
He diagnosed the problem as
    a chronic diaper rash.
He made his way back to his stand
    to scratch and yank and pull,
No doubt he was allergic to
    reprocessed Turkish wool.

His polypropyhic T-shirt that
    was bought because it breathes,
Was cold and wet and shivering
    and holding back a sneeze.
The thing that nearly killed him though
    that almost done him in,
The crotch of his new long johns
    has shrunk up to his chin.

Lester's New Longjohns

LESTER'S WARDROBE

He headed back to camp at noon
    was greeted by the group,
"Hey Les, you're like a noodle
    in a bowl of chicken soup."
Frozen, soaked, and miserable
    Old Les had had enough,
And headed back to Goodwill
    to pick up all his stuff.

"I'm sorry friend, your stuff is gone
    some guy from out-of-state,
He took it all for five bucks
    and he said your stuff was great.
He traded in his checkered greens
    and took your gear instead,
His state had passed a law that said
    Its hunters must wear Red."

"And by the way, you should have read
    that new law over twice,
You would have found in fine print
    That half orange would suffice.
Say Pal, it looks, like my remarks
    have caused you some dismay,
I only meant, you could have used, your old Reds anyway."

The Monster Recreated

Since the year they married, with the first chill fall wind
She'd watch as her husband's depression set in
From the time the first leaf fell, till the branches were bare
She'd watch his mood change, and his blank vacant stare.

His shoulders would droop, and he'd walk with a shuffle
His speech incoherent, he'd talk in a muffle
It was only at full rut, that he might wear a smile
As he'd watch two bucks race, 'cross the back quarter mile.

For a hunter he'd been, till he'd taken his vow
But the farm and his family took all his time now
His rifle unused, bore a fine coat of rust
In the closet his hunting coat covered with dust.

For nearly a year now she'd worked out a plan
How this season she'd have a surprise for her man
She knew a vacation could do him no harm
And she'd kept careful notes how to run the whole farm.

At breakfast one morning, she said, "There's no reason
Why you can't go up North for the deer hunting season
To the shack with your friends, to enjoy your old sport
I'll stay home with the cows, and hold down the fort."

He snapped to attention, and blurted out, "Why?"
And she thought she detected a tear in his eye
"Are you sure you can do it, Wow! That'd be great,
I miss it up North so, I hardly can wait."

Immediate happy, good natured was he
Total loss of depression, from what she could see
While he worked, he did whistle, and hum a nice tune
And skipped to the house for his lunch right at noon.

The Friday 'fore season, t'was time to be going
He asked her once more, "Are you sure what you're doing?"
She replied ever sweetly, "Nine days isn't long,
And with my preparation, what would ever go wrong?"

The evening chores done, she headed for bed
Alone it would be such a long day ahead
She awoke about midnight, as a blizzard blew in
As she peered out the window, the yard light went dim.

THE MONSTER RECREATED

The power was out! Oh, what would she do?
She'd have to start milking by five, that she knew
For the cows they were used to a certain routine
To expect them to change would be cruel and quite mean.

The flashlight she needed, in deer camp instead
Through the dark she did feel her way to the shed
To locate and start the reserve generator
Had she known what she'd find, she'd have gone out much later.

The shed door was frozen as tight as a tick
She proceeded to free it, on the thirty-ninth kick
As she pushed the door open, she dropped her fur mitten
She bent down, and picked up, a small striped kitten.

"Odoriferous One"

SOME OF THE GANG

Well the skunk did its thing on her new overalls
The proximity caused quite a few tears to fall
The tractor reluctant, did finally go
To the parlor she headed through ice and the snow.

The odor caused Bossy's big eyeballs to roll
Milk production that morning, took a terrible toll
As she unhooked the milker, from cow thirty-four
It struck her she'd milked this same cow before.

The cows had walked circles, a really neat trick
Instead of being done, she'd only milked six
By the time she was done, it was quarter past ten
It wouldn't be long, she'd be milking again.

Breathe Deep Girls. there's Enough to go around.

She'd have to hand feed them, right from the start
Unable to push, the old silage cart
She'd have to carry bales, the snow drifts to fight
The door to the loft was completely stuck tight.

She paused for a breather, and a first ever view
From on top of a silo, what else can one do?
The silo unloader, she unstuck with ease
But on the way down, her ears they did freeze.

Such a morning it seems, would make most women sputter
As she stood staring now, at a nearly full gutter
The bull it just missed, but one cat it did maim
The projectile known, as a barn cleaner chain.

SOME OF THE GANG

The spreader was frozen, the tractor was stuck
The barnyard a quagmire, of mud and such yuck
The thought just alone, could blow anyone's cork
Nine days of barn cleaning, with a short-handled fork.

The driveway was plugged, compressor burned out
No one to turn to, makes anyone shout
The water pipes frozen, beginning to leak
The wind and the snow, makes the barn rafters creak.

It'd been thirty six hours since she'd last seen a bed
On the pillow she gently had lowered her head
But her nostrils detected, the faint smell of smoke
From a sound sleep, she sat up, fully awoke.

To unplug a chimney should be no big trick
But she did not account for a roof which was slick
Add an improper angle, to the lean of a ladder
As she straddled midair, things couldn't be sadder.

THE MONSTER RECREATED

A thought crossed her mine, spread eagle up there
Of what happens when people do splits in the air
If the ladder slips more, how the neighbors will laugh
When her husband speaks fondly, of his wife's better half.

And so the days passed, till the season was done
And her husband returned from the nine days of fun
He hugged her and said, "I can't thank you enough
The rest did me good, the camp life and stuff.

And the gang all declared, that you must be a queen
You're something beyond their wildest dream.
And Honey, guess what, the last news is best.
They've invited me hunting, next month, way out West."

The Revenge of Ralph the Camp Cook

Each season Ralph goes early, just to get the camp in shape
He sweeps out all the cobwebs, and dusts the tattered drapes
He splits the cookstove wood fine, has the evening meat cooked
The camp is warm and comfy, not a thing Ralph overlooks.

Last season started out the same, as some twenty seasons past
But the friendly way it started out, just somehow wouldn't last
Cause as we all arranged our gear, so in the morning we'd be ready
Weak-Eyes entered the door and said, "Boys,
    this is my brother-in-law Freddy."

THE REVENGE OF RALPH THE CAMP COOK

Well if first impression we should take
Of our uninvited, new campmate
As he hauled in his gear, our hearts just sunk
He threw stuff on, and claimed, Ralph's very own bunk.

Then Fred's voice from the back said, "Your roof must leak some,
There's ice on my blankets, on the bedpost some gum.
My pillow's not fluffy, the place smells like mice
Weak-Eyes had told me, your camp was so nice."

Ralph cringed when he heard this, but said not one word
But from the kitchen an audible growl could be heard
And as Ralph set the table, the dishes slammed down
Ralph's warm friendly smile, was replaced by a frown.

Ralph then called supper, the first there was Fred
Who took Ralph's seat at the table, not the side, but the head
Took most of the taters, three choice cuts of meat
Used Ralph's shirt for a napkin, and proceeded to eat.

SOME OF THE GANG

Now Fred might have been Weak-Eye's wife's only brother
But his remarks on Ralph's food, came one after the other.
"Hey Ralph, did you get these spuds from a box?
The gravy's like water, from old athletic socks."

"This horsemeat I'm eating, what was it's name?
It's burned like the old nag, backed into a flame.
I'd take scraps to my dog, but I'd hate to offend her
And the coffee is cold, but at least it is tender."

Each callous remark, made Ralph shudder a bit
And we figured that Fred, was about to get hit.
How Ralph kept his cool, is beyond my belief
When Fred belched and said, "Ralph, how do *you* spell relief?"

When supper was over, we headed for bed
Then a remark that Ralph made once, shot through my head.
"Life's too short to get angry, it's my one firm believin'
I'll never get mad, but you can bet I'll get even."

The springs 'neath the mattresses, squeaked as we turned
While Ralph worked in the kitchen, my suspicions confirmed,
Ralph's way to get even, if I had my hunch
Would be met as Ralph packed, each man a lunch.

Fred slept straight through breakfast of pancakes and steak
When he finally got up, we had fast tracks to make.
"With no food I can't make it" Fred said in demand,
"Ralph *better* have fixed me, a lunch for my stand."

Ralph dropped off Fred, at the Frozen Crow Stand,
Reached three miles through swamp, or two miles by land.
"You're first off in the morning, the last one we'll get,
Be ready for pick up, just before the sun sets."

SOME OF THE GANG

Fred reached the stand by way of the marsh
He stood sweaty but chilled, as the cold wind blew harsh
"I'm so starved and so cold, it's a good thing for me,
Ralph packed me some sandwiches, and strong hot coffee."

The sack Fred then opened, inside he could see,
Ralph's hand written message addressed just to he.
"My supper last evening, perhaps was too plain,
Inside are some delicacies, you should not complain."

The thermos was full, but of cold mushroom soup
Fred's stomach made one quick, aerial loop.
A sandwich wrapped up, in aluminum foil
Consisted of sardines, in iced soybean oil.

Frantically, Fred reached for another
Liver on which, greasy onions did smother
The last one was soggy, of garlic did reek,
From which Limburger cheese, with much ketchup did peek.

One last container, way down at the bottom
From a crack in its cover, came odors quite rotten
Fred lifted the corner, one look was enough
Last week's taco salad, garnished with snuff.

Fred's eyes did a slow spin, his stomach did flips
The hunger pangs reached from his throat to his hips
Fred's cold trembling fingers, held a note which he read
"You connoisseurs may like this, I like plain foods instead."

When Ralph picked Fred up, he lay prone in the ditch
His eyes searched for food, like a mad man bewitched
Fred groped for the door handle, then slid in the seat
As they drove into camp, not one word did they speak.

At the table for supper, Fred sat at the side
And his fondness for Ralph's food, he just couldn't hide
When finished he said, "Ralph, it was simply delicious
would you mind if I helped you do the night's dishes?"

Whitetail Barney's Buddy

T'was near the end of last July,
when Barney's wife she asked him why
He had to head for camp at noon,
his mother-in-law would visit soon.

"I know, said he, "it is too bad,
again to miss her makes me sad."
He quickly turned his head in fear,
she'd see him grin from ear to ear.

"Tell her business calls me North,
I must scout deer trails and so forth,
I must keep food here on the table,
and must do so whenever able."

With that he jumped into his Scout,
to pick up Weak-Eyes while enroute.
Their talk had turned as camp drew near
to the upcoming season for hunting deer.

Barney said, "My thrill would be
if in the record book I'd see
My name beside a record buck,
if only I could have such luck."

The road to camp passed Barney's stand,
t'was nearly dusk, when from a popple stand
Stepped a ghostly buck with velvet rack
and twenty points, now that's a fact.

"It's him! It's him!" poor Barney screamed,
"The record whitetail of my dreams,
At rutting time, should he act dumb,
it's Boone and Crockett, here I come."

Elated, they turned in the drive,
and the headlights showed a thing alive.
Sat perched up in the buck-pole tree,
a porcupine they both could see.

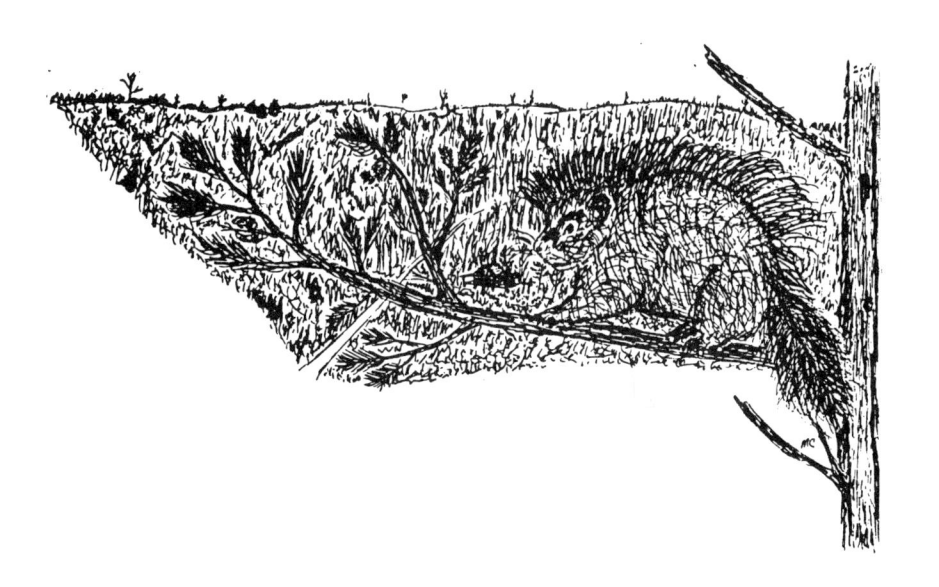

Weak-Eyes said, "Hand me the gun,
I'll blow that thing to Kingdom Come.
He'll eat his way into our shack
and have it gone time we get back."

Barney spoke straight from his heart
"Weak-Eyes," he said, "I'll have no part
In senseless killing and the like,
just let the Porky take a hike."

SOME OF THE GANG

Time did pass, and opening morn,
found Barney on his stump adorn,
In Fluorescent coat and buck-rut lure
he felt his buck would show for sure.

A twig then snapped, which caught his ear,
he sensed his record buck draw near.
A perfect shot, his dream fullfilled,
a world record he had killed.

At camp it took all six of us
to get the buck hung high enough
Protected up the buck-pole tree
for all the other camps to see.

Next morning the alarm did ring,
and Barney from his bunk did spring,
Said, "Boys I'm headed out to see,
my record whitetail in the buck-pole tree."

We heard him gasp, and then scream,
we all sensed trouble, but didn't dream,
We'd witness what we all did see,
as we assembled 'neath the buck-pole tree.

There below his big buck's feet
lay a pile of antler chips, two feet deep,
The record horns were chewed up fine,
Porky'd gnawed them to the buck's hairline.

His shoulders slumped, tears filled his eyes,
"That porcupine I do despise."
The Porky grinned from up the tree,
then Barney said, "It's him or me."

The Porky knew his time was up,
and scrambled toward the very top.
With Barney closing in behind,
hand over head up the tall jack pine.

They reached the peak, the tree did sway,
a sudden snap as the top gave way.
Limbs, cones, and needles, long johns and quills
fell so fast to the ground, that it gave us the chills.

Barney hit ground with a terrible thud
and staggered to his feet in the snow and mud.
Then leveled a kick at the fat Porky's rear,
with precision that would make a place kicker cheer.

The Porky sailed high,
o'er the tall cabin's peak.
Then Barney let out a bloodcurdling shriek.
He hopped and he jumped and let out with a hoot,
with 96 quills buried deep in his boot.

It was 14 miles to the nearest doc,
who surgically removed poor Barney's sock.
Doc said, "Hang on, there's more to go,"
then pulled 25 quills from Barney's big toe.

On the way back to camp, Barney didn't say much.
And he limped as he walked from the car with his crutch,
Insult to injury, a warden said, "Here,"
and fined Barney for shooting an anterless deer.

This sad tale is over. The trophy is gone.
Just a thing to remember as years pass along.
But over his mantel, instead of his kill,
hangs Barney's old boot,
covered with quills.

The Old Forkhorn Insurance Company, Inc.
SINCE 1976

Protection Designed for the Outdoorsman

EFFECTIVE DATE:
This agreement is effective upon receipt of the application and enrollment fee. It remains in force for 12 months (or one year) whichever occurs first. Coverage is automatically renewable at the end of each yearly enrollment period unless you have attempted to claim benefits during the past year.

SCHEDULE OF BENEFITS
The following benefits are provided by this Agreement for the treatment of accidental injury or death sustained by the enrollee(s) during legal hunting hours and after hour activities occurring between 9:00 PM and 2:00 AM only.

1. Surgical care:
    rendered by a licensed physician or the camp cook including:
    — appendectomies
    — tonsil removal
    — perforating ear drums
    — tapping clogged nasal passages
    — removal of deer hooves-oral removal only
    — repacking hemorrhoids-(camp cook will share expenses with Old Forkhorn)
    — ingrown toenail removal-left foot only
    — removal of a maimed limb-covered only when removed in pairs
    — open heart surgery-covered only when deemed necessary by the camp cook
    — closing of open wounds caused by goring
    — stitching of oral opening-covered when enrollee is unanimously considered the camp loudmouth
    — stitching cut on brow or forehead-if caused by recoil of scoped rifle
    — removal of a buck tag from achilles tendon
    — any case of malnutrition for being unable to eat the cooks food

HOSPITAL SERVICES
OFIC will reimburse the enrollee(s) for the actual cost of hospital care not to exceed 150 times the cost of enrollment for any one accidental injury and/or one death provided that such hospital care is necessary.

If death occurs more than once to an enrollee(s) during the course of one hunting season (1year), benefits will not be provided by Old Forkhorn.

COVERED AMOUNTS
OFIC will pay in full up to 150 times the enrollment fee the usual, customary, and reasonable area fees for surgical care provided by a licensed participating physician or camp cook. (However, very few claims as such can be considered reasonable.)
If the attending physician will not accept payment for benefit claims from OFIC, you will consider yourself SOL or Up a Creek. If such an event occurs a paddle will be provided by Old Forkhorn.

DURATION OF BENEFITS
In order to be covered by this Agreement an injury or death must occur within the term of the Agreement and related treatment of such injury or death must be started within 180 days.

LIMITATIONS AND EXCLUSIONS
The benefits offered by this Agreement are subject to the limitations and exclusions referred to herein.
A. Benefits will not be provided for expenses required to treat the following:
  1. the removal of porcupine quills imbedded in an outhouse
  2. infection by poison ivy caused when the use of leaves was deemed necessary by the enrollee
  3. cabin fever-no one said you had to stay so long
  4. ptomaine poisoning from attending a buoya
  5. amputation of or the application of a cast on a phalange (hand or foot) injured by being stepped on while attending a Hunter's Ball
  6. stitches required to close any wound inflicted during a bar room brawl
  7. indigestion caused by the swallowing of any labels from bottles, flip tops, gum wrappers, forks or cartridges
  8. treatment for headache or nauseaa-that's your own fault
  9. treatment for smoke inhalation from a backed up wood range
  10. the removal and/or repair of broken teeth caused by misplacing the bottle opener
  11. the removal of splinters and/or saplings falling from a tree stand
  12. severe cases of Montezuma's revenge due to the overeating of fresh venison liver and onions
  13. treatment of crotch rot or chaffing
  14. the surgical removal of long johns worn all season
  15. separation of and resulting treatment for gummed armpits
  16. crimes of passion as a direct result of wearing buck scent
  17. burns and/or blisters caused by sitting on your handwarmer

If an erollee(s) is severely injured or killed by another he should report such injury or death to Old Forkhorn as soon as possible in order for policy termination to begin immediately.

D.R. Droppings-Vice-President
Delbert W.W. Forkhorn-President
Rut N. Season-Agent
Bernie Brushbuster-Agent

Jay Camprobber-Secretary
Andrew Antlers-Assoc. Vice President
Minnie Bucks-Treasurer
Lotsa Doe-Assistant Treasurer

INVOLUNTARY SPORTSMEN'S LICENSE

Get Permission to Trespass

TO: LAST NAME

FIRST NAME

Involuntary Contribution: FREE

Issued By: _____

Date: _____

PLACE PARTY PERMIT STAMP HERE	PLACE BUCK FAWN STAMP HERE
PLACE DOE FAWN STAMP HERE	PLACE ADULT DOE STAMP HERE
PLACE SPIKE BUCK STAMP HERE	PLACE FORK BUCK STAMP HERE

PLACE ADDITIONAL STAMPS HERE

New Rules At A Glance

Hunters must be aware of the new rules and regulations which go into effect this year.

HUNTING METHOD RESTRICTIONS

You May Not:
a. discharge a firearm in a moving vehicle
b. leave home without your weapon
c. fall asleep on a stand
d. snap twigs while sneak hunting
e. damage or destroy the leaves, branches, bark, or trunk of any state

owned tree with a ricochet
f. eject more than three unfired shells in a row at the sight of a buck
g. place any snare, snake pit, spear or gill net on any trail used by deer
h. take sound shots between 6:30 a.m. and 4:30 p.m.
i. trip, slip, slide, or fall over a brush pile
j. use during the rut as live bait, a doe weighing less than 140 lbs.
k. shoot a deer in bed
l. tow a canoe through the woods containing more than seven occupants

POSSESSION AND DISPOSITION RESTRICTIONS

You May Not:

a. Remove steaks and/or other portions from the hindquarter of the campmeat carcass between the hours of 11:59 P.M. and 12:00 A.M. daily.
b. Hang or display from a buck pole any red squirrel, blue jay, snowshoe hare, or porcupine unless such animal has been tagged in such a manner that the removal of such tag is impossible.
c. Fire an excess of two full clips or magazines into the hindquarter of your buck that has just been tagged by another.
d. Use a fingernail clipper to gut out a deer.
e. Slice steaks thicker than one-half inch.
f. Remove the heart or liver from the gut pile of another unless such pile is frozen or snow covered.

CLOTHING REQUIREMENTS

You May Not:

a. Wear or carry any belt-type knife exceeding the length of your feet unless wearing suspenders.
b. Stray, wander, or walk off any established trail or forest road if your boot size exceeds 14D.
c. Carry tubes of Chapstick or ballpoint pens in your shell pocket.
d. Sew your back tag to your shorts.
e. Sew the back flap of another's one piece long john's shut.
f Wear your boots on the wrong feet.

RESTRICTION ON CAMP LIFE
You May Not:
a. Make obscene remarks or gestures to members of neighboring camps that have more deer on their buck pole.
b. Exceed a speed limit of 10 mph on a trip to the outhouse.
c. Leave a stander out all day as a practical joke.
d. Borrow or attempt to steal buck lure belonging to another.
e. Carry an intoxicated member of your camp to his stand.
f. Store buck lure in a syrup bottle.

GENERAL RESTRICTIONS
You May Not:
a. Use a hacksaw having more than 24 teeth per inch for the removal of antlers from winter kills.
b. Use a spotlight, jacklight, or hand held lantern to harass or attempt to drive off a warden.
c. Use any rope, hemp, twine, or steel cable larger than one-half inch in diameter to aid in the removal of a deer from its place of demise.
d. Walk in circles when lost.
e. Pour, spray, or spill essence of skunk oil on any article of clothing 3 hours prior to entering any camp.
f. Cough, wheeze, gasp, or sneeze within 200 yards of another hunter.
g. Scream if gored by a buck.
h. Be kicked in the groin by a wounded deer.
i. Walk through a woods backwards.
j. Brush, blow, remove, or melt the snow from any log or stump you wish to sit on.

You Will be Allowed to:
a. Have fun, be careful, and get your buck this year.

Should he elude you
 Don't grieve and despair
In his woods you're a stranger
 He's spent his Life there.
           Cowley '82'

A Deerhunter's Prayer

Lord, let there be a tracking snow
    to help me get my buck
And let my aim be straight and true
    to aid me in my luck
And when the time has come, Lord
    that ends my Northwoods tromp
Let me hear just one more time
    "It's daylight in the swamp."

—Cowley '79

You drove my wife and kids
up to camp as a joke?

Get over here quick!
Your long johns are trying to
crawl across the floor.

Anybody seen the gun oil?
 I had it in an old syrup bottle.

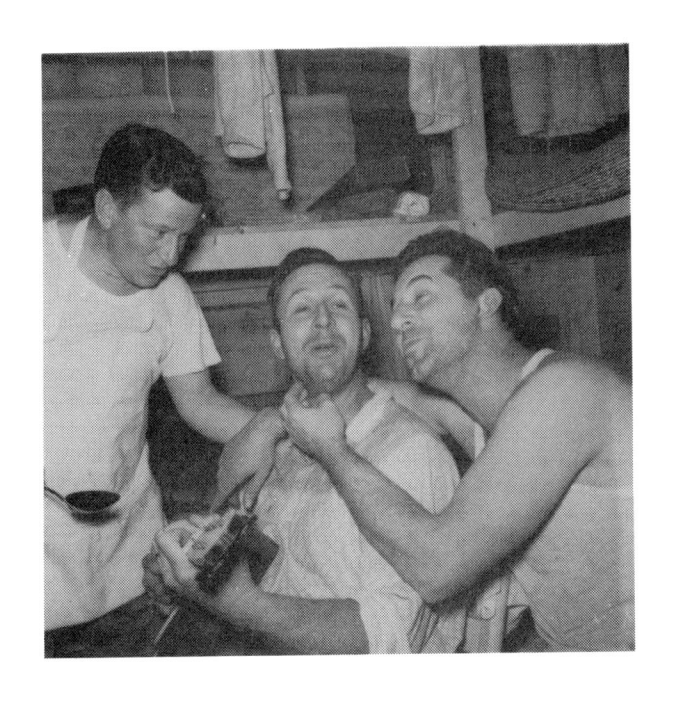

Which one of you guys is singing soprano?

SOME OF THE HUNTS

The Ultimate Stand

He'd spent several hours, seated right on the ground
A bitter cold wind blew, that muffled all sound
He shuddered from chill, his teeth chattered a bit
But on opening morning, there was no way he'd quit.

It appeared as a gray ghost, midst a swirl of snow
The escape route past Barney, he'd chosen to go
The buck's polished antlers, six tines on each side
For a few precious yards had nowhere to hide.

THE ULTIMATE STAND

Barney tried a shot seated, but he shook from the cold
On its shoulder, his front sight, he just couldn't hold
As he squeezed off the first round, his shot went too high
And the old buck dug in, nearly starting to fly.

Then Barney tried standing, but too stiff from the cold
A tale of misery, began to unfold
He tried one more shot, but in vain he could tell
As the buck, in a few leaps, went over the hill.

It was over in seconds, Barney started to shake
His ground stand was more, than his body could take
To himself made a vow, "This won't happen again,
By next year I'll create, The Ultimate Stand."

THE ULTIMATE STAND

From that moment on, hunter now turned inventor
Spent his time drawing blueprints, round the stand life did center
"My stand will have comforts, never thought of by man,
No cost shall be spared on, The Ultimate Stand."

"My stand, when complete, will be a true masterpiece
I'll be known worldwide, from Glen Flora to Greece
I'll retire and travel, speak to groups far and near
There'll be a battle for sales, from Montgomery and Sears."

Such thoughts spurred him on, restless was he
Gathering parts and small pieces, all he could see
Buying and bagging, from the junkyard he'd get
Not an auction or yard sale, did he fail to hit.

His materials gathered, he checked over his list
To make absolute sure, there was no part he'd missed
From the dentist, a chair, and two old dental tools
And a ball bearing base from a bartender's stool
His wife's orange umbrella, in case of a rain,
And a switch and transformer, from his son's Lionel train
A seat belt and dash from his brother's old van
Parts from a Maytag, that no longer ran
A dual heat blanket, a garage sale gem
And for power, the battery, from his old Farmall M.

Once assembly was started, nothing got in his way
He worked in his shop, through the night and all day
He forgot his wife's birthday, the lawn went unmowed
It was July when he noticed, the oats were not sowed.

He worked like a madman, a deadline to meet
He barely took time out to eat or to sleep
The stand should be given, a full field test
But as November approached, he had no time to rest.

As the last nut was tightened, the soldering done
Barney opened the shop doors, to the new morning sun
There'd be no time to test it, but with faith in his plan,
Tomorrow he'd hunt from, "The Ultimate Stand."

He selected a spot overlooking a slashing
Where he'd view any deer, that was coming or passing
He set up the stand, on a tripod affair
So when seated he'd be, sixteen feet in the air.

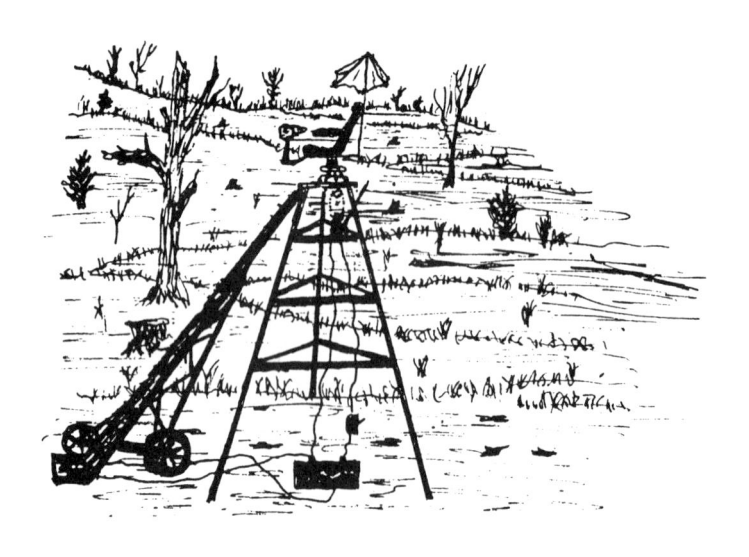

With camouflage net, to ward off detection
It'd be ready to go, with the battery connection
To protect his invention, just in case someone tried
He scratched in the words, "Patent Applied."

THE ULTIMATE STAND

Before six in the morning of opening day
To the stand in the slashing, Barney now made his way
With the flick of a switch, rode the stand's escalator
To the top, on some parts, of his hay elevator.

Barney seated himself, and started to grin
As he plugged all the electrical appliances in
To the coffee soon perked, and what he liked the most
With the heat blanket going, he was warm as some toast.

All was going well, as he surveyed the land
Barney up there, in The Ultimate Stand
When off in the distance, a deer he could see
A little to the left, about thirty degrees.

Designed so his hands would always be free
The button to Rotate, he touched with his knee
The chair slowly swiveled, to the left as you'd hope
And Barney soon had, the buck in his scope.

With the buck fully centered, in the field of view
On the shoulder, the crosshairs, held steady and true
Barney was ready, to squeeze off a shot
When the buck in the scope, suddenly was not.

The buck reappeared, then was quick gone again
This sequence occurred, again and again
Barney looked down, not deserving his fate
The Maytag's old gears were in, Agitate.

THE ULTIMATE STAND

For a second it paused, then started again
The gearbox had suddenly shifted to spin
It started out slow, moving counterclockwise
Barney's life passed before him, as terror filled his eyes.

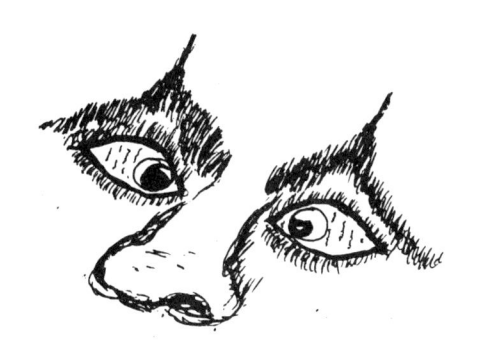

The speed seemed to increase, he continued to spin
The seat belt the only thing, holding him in
His hat and his boots, flew way off, of course,
Caused by 3g's of centrifugal force.

His hair got so stretched out, it started to ache
Blood rushed to his head till he thought it would break
Gripping the armrests, till his knuckles turned white
His hunting pants pulled off, the suspenders stretched light.

He spun like an astronaut, during rehearsal
Then felt like a watch, in a Timex commercial
Barney's poor body, kept taking a licking
As The Ultimate Stand, continued its ticking

It took nearly four hours, till the battery wore down
So he could release the seat belt, and fall to the ground
He walked like a cowboy, his legs fully bowed
As he circled each tree, between his stand and the road.

Barney never went back, to "The Ultimate Stand"
It remains in the woods, overlooking the land
Should you happen accross it, feel free to climb in
But remember, with time, batteries recharge again.

Willie and
The Aerial Drive

Reclined in this lawn chair as darkness set in
Willie did wait for the show to begin
For next to deer hunting, he did not know why
He loved fireworks on the Fourth of July.

His mind drifted back, to the deer season past
All the scouting he'd done, his stand picked at last
His predawn maneuvers, the trails he'd found
Then opening day, not a hair nor a sound.

"There must be a reason, it just isn't fair
To hunt all day long, and not see a hair.
Is it weather conditions, or plain rotten luck?
For try as I may, I just can't find a buck."

A bright flash above him, a near sonic boom
Brought him back to the present, return him his gloom.
A Roman sky rocket, had climbed out of sight
Exploding with colors, in rainbows of light.

As though struck by brilliance, he leaped to his feet
"I've a better idea, that Ford couldn't beat.
I'll not know its potential till fully explored
Why didn't I think of this method before?"

He ran to the house for a pencil to fetch
And a small pad of paper on which he could sketch.
To record his ideas, to keep them alive
All the pertinent facts, 'bout "The Aerial Drive."

He quick scribbled notes, not forgetting a one
Making certain the layout was properly done.
"In a two-mile arc, I shall run a fine wire
Then attach Roman rockets, which electrically fire
With a dynamite plunge box kept at my stand
I'll detonate charges, with the touch of my hand.
Add a few bottle rockets, a whistle thrown in
And an ambulance siren to add to the din
A Kaooga horn from an old Model A
and a Democrat poster, in hopes it will bray."

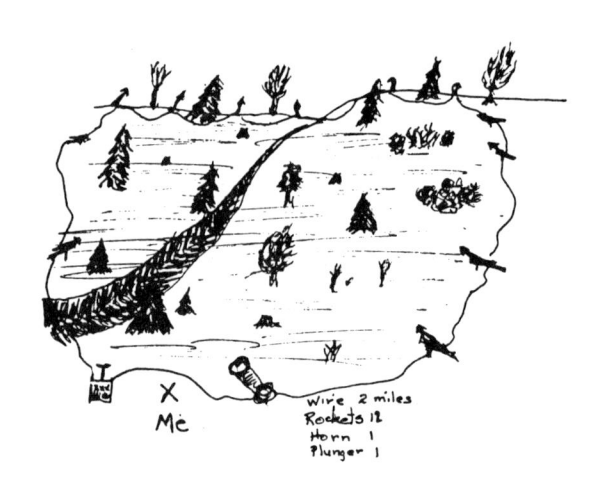

His plans etched on paper, a test must be made
So a miniature arc in his woodlot he laid
Though in much smaller scale, t'was proof that he strived
If it worked he'd perfect a large, "Aerial Drive."

Willie's wife stood beside him for moral support
Conducting the test from their new screened-in porch.
In but a few seconds, a doe and a fawn
Made good their escape, right across the front lawn.

"It works," Willie shouted, "I'm finally in luck
On a much larger scale, I'll chase out a buck."
His wife screamed, "Oh, Mercy!' and 'Land Sakes Alive!'
I've just witnessed the world's first, 'Aerial Drive.'"

Now the DNR claimed sixteen deer to the square
Willie worked with this number plus or minus a pair.
By counting his fingers, did then calculate.
Deer should pass by his stand, to the square root of eight.

Through the rest of the summer, though sultry and hot
Willie spent countless hours as he slaved in his shop.
With ramps of thick plywood, and angles just right
Elongated sections of old sewer pipe
Exhaust pipes removed from an old rusty car
And pipes from a cookstove with creosote tar.
Perfecting his launches, to be safe and strong
So on opening morning, not a thing should go wrong.

Two weeks before season he loaded his goods
And headed up north to his favorite woods
With transit in hand and geometry book
The Northwoods about to take on a new look.

From geometry class, Willie finally made use
For the sum of the sides, square the hypotenuse.
The launchers at angles precise and so fine
Mathematically proven by sine and cosine.

The rockets installed with their launchers held steady
Willie stepped back, for he knew he was ready.
Selecting the spot he would now call his stand
Hid the plungebox in leaves, so it'd be close at hand.

T'was the night before season, when all should go well
Found a wet heavy snow of ten inches that fell.
Bending down branches, and forming a tangle,
And clinging to rockets...
       and changing their angle.

Willie on stand at a quarter past six
Glanced down at his watch for those few final ticks
At exactly six thirty, the plunger went down,
From two miles away, started cannon-type sounds.

The rockets their angles, quite changed by the snow
Flew off in directions, some high and some low
Some prematurely, and some delayed action
But all, rest assured, would result in some action.

WILLIE AND THE AERIAL DRIVE

A partridge was first to succumb to a missile
When startled to flight by an ear piercing whistle.
Twisting and turning, in efforts to flee
Then breaking its neck, as it crashed in a tree.

And Fluffy, the fox squirrel, high in his nest
Had not yet awoke, from the past evening's rest.
Both he and a hunter, on stand up the tree,
Went down together, from old rocket three.

The Park Ranger, Smith, who was new on the job
Would suffer grave harm, from a misaligned lob.
Blown from his tower, swanned a hundred-foot dive
Just chalk up one more, for the "Aerial Drive."

SOME OF THE HUNTS

And Dale, the Warden, his window rolled down
Was cupping his hand to hear gunfire sounds.
Through the window, a pinwheel has a terrible effect
When attached to the back of a Game Warden's neck.

And the old Widow Brown was a mile away
Picking up wood for her cookstove that day.
When Willie's fizz rocket, did sneak up behind
Implanting itself where the sun doesn't shine.

WILLIE AND THE AERIAL DRIVE

Alerted by shouting, much cursing was heard
Willie fled from his stand, when he picked out the words.
"Where's the jerk that invented this "Aerial Drive?"
Catch up to the twit, and he'll boil alive."

Willie ran for his truck and arrived just in time
To jam it in first, leaving victims behind.
Taking the backroads, to avoid all detection
While praying they'd look, in some other direction.

He turned into camp in a full power slide
Then raced for the shack planning where he would hide
Jumped the steps in one leap, and then ran through the door
Slammed it shut, had it bolted, like never before.

The others in camp, Willie now had to face
To admit to defeat, would be total disgrace.
"Hey! Will, you surprised us. You're really back quick.
That drive you invented must really work slick."

Willie thought out his words, as he calmly said, "Yes.
You just wouldn't believe how it worked I confess.
I'll be honest and tell you, not one man alive,
Wasn't looking for me, and my "Aerial Drive."

The Dream

It seemed that Louie'd never learned
    it wasn't something new
He'd overdosed on venison
    and heaping bowls of stew
It may have been the sauerkraut
    that made him twist and turn
Or piles of buttered onions
    That had caused him grave concern.

He moaned and groaned and held his gut
    and then he said, "I bet
This pain could be attributed
    to something that I et"
He stumbled, toward his bunk and said
    "I think it might be best
If I lay down for just a while
    and catch a little rest."

We had to just ignore him
    as we played our game of cards
Though concentrating on our hands
    sometimes was really hard
But Louie scared us all that night
    when startled by his scream
The gang rushed to his bedside
    to arouse him from "The Dream."

SOME OF THE HUNTS

At first we feared a heart attack
    would claim our hunting friend
Surrounded by his campmates
    poor old Louie'd face the end
Instead old Louie sat up straight
    as beads of sweat did stream
He shook and blinked and stuttered
    as he told us of "The Dream."

"Boys, I hope you all recall
    the words that Weak-Eyes said"
"If deer were armed with rifles
    we would probably all be dead"
"Well in my dream was such a place
    it wasn't far from here
Where open season was declared
    on *men,* pursued by deer."

"There I was a huntin' from
    The trusty popple stand
Just mindin' my own business
    as I sat and watched the land
When down there in the valley
    came a terrible, ghastly sight
Two bucks pulled out this hunter
    with their drag rope stretched out tight.'

THE DREAM

One buck then told the other, "Man,
    now wasn't that a drag
Just think, it took but one shot
    from my thirty-forty Krag."
Then glancing to my left I saw
    this buck up in a tree
On stand, was watching trails with
    his new two forty three."

"Believe me I got out of there
    as quickly as I could
I thought I'd find some safety
    if I hid out in the woods
About the time I thought perhaps
    I'd make it out alive
I'd run smack in the middle of
    a terrible ten deer drive!"

"I then ran down a trail that
    was narrow but was straight
Trying to dodge the bullets from
    a lever three-O-eight
I knew right then I had to find
    a brand-new bag of tricks
when this buck picked up my trail
    with a fancy scoped ot-six."

SOME OF THE HUNTS

"I hid then in some alders as
    I tried to catch my breath
And thanked my lucky stars so far
    I had avoided death
When several bucks came into view
    just out to have some fun
They thought they'd make a sport of it
    with old blackpowder guns."

"Then on stand there stood a buck
    with horns grown quite immense
I hurt myself severely as
    I jumped a barbed wire fence
I woke up when I heard him say,"
    "Look here, a fresh blood trail
And judging by the track size
    I would guess that it's a male."

Our gang has little sympathy
    but offered him assurance
We told him that he might feel better
    if he carried good insurance
We did insist he listen when
    we offered this suggestion
"Louie, don't take naps no more
    when you suffer indigestion."

The Bog

With cautious steps, the Old Buck worked
    his way through knee-deep snow
The ancient path he followed
    left by deer from long ago.
The trail turned, then left the ridge
    of scrub oak, winding slow
Down the slope, into the swamp
    and alder patch below.

The hunter, Charlie, took the trail
    and to himself he grinned
He'd had bucks take this trail before
    and every time he'd win.
His method proven, many times
    he'd parallel the side
In ambush lay, he'd take the buck
    as in the brush he'd hide.

THE SERIOUS SIDE

The buck, himself an elder
    he was aged as far as deer
Had sensed that he was followed
    when Old Charlie'd gotten near.
He turned and trained his amble ears
    and strained for every sound.
That'd warn him when, the near approach
    of danger was around.

Old Charlie in the meantime
    had decided where he'd hide
And lay in silent ambush
    with the alders at his side.
If things worked as he figured
    as in countless seasons past
The trail used by this Old Buck
    quite soon would be it's last.

As minutes passed, and time flew by
    no buck was there around
Old Charlie felt a chill set in
    while lying on the ground.
Cramped and stiff, he finally stood
    when he could take no more
And realized he'd never dealt
    with such a buck before.

As Charlie stretched his legs he thought
    "I'll go and take the track,
And see which way the old boy heads.
    Tomorrow I'll be back."
He studied hard, the tracks he found
    which told him quite a tale,
"That Old Buck *knew* where I would be
    as I waited on his trail."

THE SERIOUS SIDE

He had but just an hour left
      till darkness settled in
He'd mark the track, and in the morn,
      he'd pick it up again.
A short cut to the ridge he'd take
      to save a lengthy jog
It'd take him through the quagmire
      and the shaky, frozen bog.

Though cautious were, the steps he took
      the ground ahead would quake
As waves of vegetation spread
      with every step he'd take
And all this time his mind was on
      The buck that'd led him here
"A buck, that smart, just *has* to be
      a very special deer."

Deep snow and stress has caused a sweat
    that trickled down his spine
He wondered why he liked these swamps
    instead of stands of pine.
He paused to glance ahead to see
    how far he had to go
There, less than fifty yards ahead
    stood the buck, in knee-deep snow.

The buck caught Charlie unprepared
    for ready, he was not
He shifted all his weight at once
    to just get off a shot.
No warning was he given
    as the roots beneath his feet
Tore, and ripped, then broke in half
    and Charlie dropped waist deep.

The icy waters, 'neath the bog
      near freezing, took his breath
His first concern was getting out
      no thought was there of death.
He reached to grab a clump of grass
      which iced, slipped through his grip
Then from his frozen fingers, watched
      his father's rifle slip.

He broke through to his arm pits with
      a sudden jolting splash
His head beneath the waters
      for an instant made him gasp
His lungs sucked tannic waters, with
      suspended bits within
Now overcome by fear of death
      his eyes began to dim.

THE BOG

The nauseating smell of muck
      the taste clung to his lips
His beard, now iced with 'cicles
      water dripping from their tips
One last attempt, his death throe
      which would sap his strength and might
It'd be but in a moment
      and he'd slowly sink from sight.

One night in camp he'd told the guys
      "When it's my time to go,
What better place than on a hunt
      in fluffy drifts of snow?"
"Not here," he thought, "this dreadful tomb,
      of darkened waters deep
Will claim me for a thousand years
      This bog, my life, will keep."

THE SERIOUS SIDE

Through clouded eyes, he peered ahead
    not knowing what there'd be
"What's that up there? Why that Old Buck
    he's staring, watching me!
I'll bet he led me here to die
    I hope he's had his thrill."
The Old Buck turned, and disappeared
    as deer so often will.

His time was near, and Charlie's arms
    began to toss and flail
His hands reached for assistance
    but they searched to no avail.
When suddenly a sapling tree
    bent down into his hand
A tiny tree, with frail roots
    but anchored to the land.

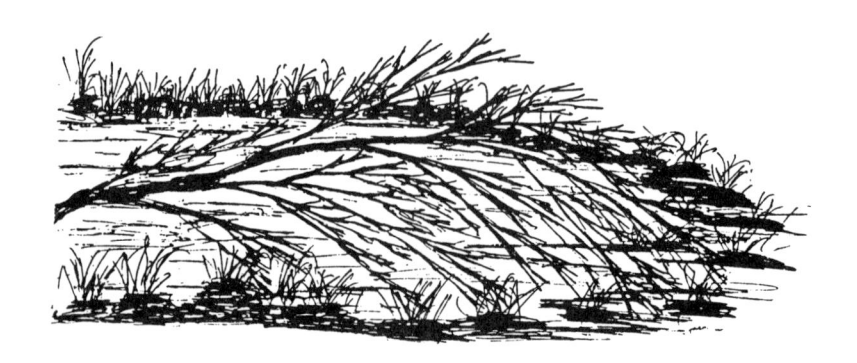

Old Charlie pulled and struggled
    as he tugged with all his might
And slid himself upon the bog
    as day now turned to night
He knew to live, he'd have to move
    and struggled to his feet
And made his way, back into camp
    exhausted, fell asleep.

Two days in camp, he had to spend
    before his strength was back
At dawn he reached and took a borrowed
    rifle from the rack
"I'll work my way into the swamp.
    "The Bog," I'll hunt once more
Today I think, that buck and I
    will even up the score."

THE SERIOUS SIDE

>He jumped the buck not far from where
>>he'd almost met the end
>And Charlie now in hot pursuit
>>possessed the upper hand
>"I'll dog this buck until he drops
>>I'll wear him to the ground
>He'll likely be, the finest buck
>>for many miles around."

>Charlie'd watch for tracks that told
>>The buck was moving fast
>He'd double time his own pace
>>and he'd slowly close the gap
>And if the buck would circle
>>watch it's trail from a bed
>Old Charlie'd slowly sneak hunt
>>Watch for movement far ahead.

Two hours of this steady chase
    The buck began to tire
Both age and wounds take heavy toll
    despite a strong desire
The Old Buck turned and caught a glimpse
    of Charlie close behind
And thought, "This man's of different stuff
    Than other men you find."

The Old Buck tried his last resort
    a method used by few
With careful steps, walked backwards
    then jumped sideways, out of view
Shaken when he watched as Charlie
    ruined his master plan
The Old Buck turned, and worked his way
    into "The Bog" again.

THE SERIOUS SIDE

    Down in the bog, the tired buck
        felt safe enough to rest
    He'd bed among the deadfalls
        to make Charlie pass the test
    He lay beside a tamarack
        a twig then snapped again
    He bolted at a movement
        it was Charlie closin' in!

    Charlie heard a ruckus come
        from somewhere up ahead
    This time it wasn't Charlie
        it was now the buck instead
    With frenzied bawls, the plea for life
        That comes from deep within
    The frantic pawing of the buck
        just sunk him deeper in.

Old Charlie closed the distance 'tween
         the predator and prey
"I've gotch'ya where I want'cha now
         you cannot get away"
Then Charlie pulled the rifle up
         and cocked the hammer back
The front sight resting steady
         on the neck, below the rack.

A millisecond separates
         a life, and then a death
The squeezing of a finger
         That would silence every breath
Old Charlie sighed, and took the gun
         and easied the hammer down
Then picked a spot, and gently lay
         The rifle on the ground.

THE SERIOUS SIDE

Charlie'd spied the sapling
    which for now stood straight and true
And with his hand, pressed on his knee
    he snapped it right in two
Then from his pocket took his rope
    with which he made a loop
When fastened to the sapling
    made a perfect snaring hoop.

The buck exhausted prostrate lay
    This last ordeal done
And from its horns Old Charlie took
    The rope, and grabbed his gun
"Take care Old Buck," as Charlie winked
    "In camp I'll take the log
And write you down, like other bucks
    I've taken from, "The Bog.""

The Rub

A tiny seed on fluffy down
    had drifted through the air
Just one of countless thousands
    set free without a care
It drifted half a mile away
    from where it was released
T'was evening till the winds died down
    before its voyage ceased.

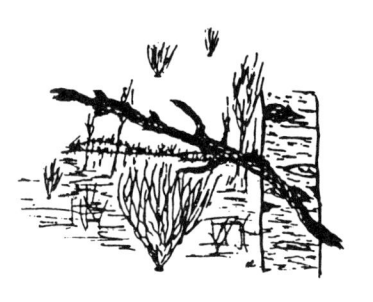

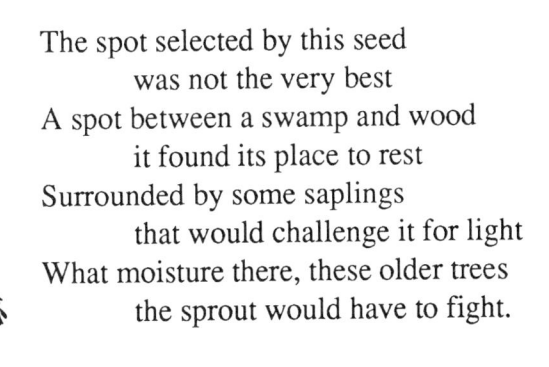

The spot selected by this seed
    was not the very best
A spot between a swamp and wood
    it found its place to rest
Surrounded by some saplings
    that would challenge it for light
What moisture there, these older trees
    the sprout would have to fight.

THE SERIOUS SIDE

    The first year found it dormant
        while protected by its coat
    The odds of its survival
        were not good and quite remote
    It must avoid detection
        from the mice and countless birds
    Or the rustle of its autumn leaves
        just never would be heard.

It sprouted in its second year
    its growth was very fast
It soon outgrew the older trees
    their height now it surpassed
Its roots could now draw moisture
    from some twenty feet away
It crowded out the smaller trees
    this sprout was here to stay.

THE RUB

The tree looked like the others
      for no difference could you find
A copy of the parent tree
      a clone among its kind
It'd live and die, and fall here
      and decay when it was dead
It'd spend its time unnoticed
      and would never turn a head.

But early one September morn
      its very trunk was shook
A casual passerby had stopped
      to take a closer look
The upper limbs they quivered
      being shaken from below
Its bark for three feet up
      was split with every blow.

THE SERIOUS SIDE

    The knife-like points did penetrate
        and cause the bark to split
    The twisting, clashing, massive horns
        then caused the bark to rip
    The assailant never did give up
        its awesome crazed-like fight
    Until one side of this young tree
        was polished clean and white.

THE RUB

The next day came and two walked by
    a hunter and his son
Out to scout for deer signs
    and enjoy the outdoor fun
"Hey, Dad, that tree, what's wrong with it?
    It looks like it's ripped up."
"Well son, you see, a great big buck
    chose it for his rub."

The Scrape

I started on my morning walk
    as dawn began to break
A trail predetermined
    the direction I would take
It led me down a valley
    which was white with autumn frost
Then wound its way back up a hill
    to a field I would cross.

Perhaps it was the broken twig
    suspended, hanging there
Or maybe unfamiliar scents
    that lingered in the air
It may have been the tine marks
    that were scratched deep in the ground
Or leaves that rustled in the wind
    with crunching walking sounds.

THE SCRAPE

For something drew my focus
        like a magnet to this spot
So barren, black, and musty
        like some secret hidden plot
He'd chosen this location
        to attract an unknown mate
And I had come upon this place
        perhaps by luck or fate.

A better view I wanted as
        I knelt to take a look
I wished not to disturb it
        so I placed each step I took
The canopy above me
        formed a shadowed leafy shrine
I felt I should not be here
        this was his place, 'twas not mine.

THE SERIOUS SIDE

He purposely had scratched off
    all the leaves, the grass, and bark
Then carefully had autographed
    his work, a print, his mark
He'd finished off his masterpiece
    with gentle strokes of horn
Then with his scent he claimed this place
    for others he would warn.

THE SCRAPE

I never got to see him
> but I knew that he was there
As he blended in the shadows
> I was pierced by his stare
I left as quickly as I came
> a different route I'd take
Should I return another day
> I'll leave alone his scrape.

THE SERIOUS SIDE

My Hunting Pardner

The cabin seemed so empty
        as I stood there by the door
Surrounded by a loneliness
        I'd never felt before
A million memories...flashing by
        of good times we had there
Then I stared beside the table
        at his dusty, empty chair.

He bought my first wool-hunting coat,
        back then a shade of red
A shiny new brass compass
        that I carry with me yet.
A hunting knife with leather case
        to wear upon my belt.
A prouder feeling no one
        but a kid has ever felt.

It seems like only yesterday
        we loaded up our gear
But nearly forty years have passed
        since we first hunted here.
Some things one takes for granted
        like a cold November wind
That seasons last forever
        and the good times never end.

MY HUNTING PARDNER

But seasons flew by quickly
    and he slowly lost his health
But kept his sense of humor
    and his wisdom was his wealth
He parted with his rifle when
    he found it of no use
Made sure it was his grandsons
    who would cause it no abuse.

I know we'll never plan a hunt
    or pack for camp again
And when I get my buck
    I'll never see his wink and grin
Although I know it's over
    but for one thing I am glad
I had the chance, and took the time
    to tell him, "Thank you, Dad."

THE SERIOUS SIDE

Remember son ...
There's a lot more to deer hunting
than going home with a buck.

A happy time in camp. Everyone is issued clean underwear!

Serious business 'neath the dim corner light.

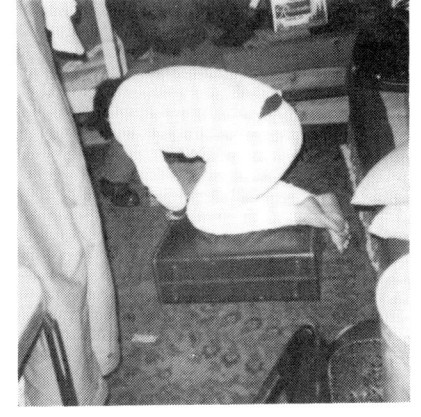

Somebody help me. My buck tag's in here.

Was this buck taken on "The Aerial Drive?"

2 on the pole are worth 3 in the brush.

129

Pearly Camp #1, 1976.

Two on Thanksgiving Day, 1981.

Four from one stand isn't bad, but he missed one besides

*Dan with a good hand.
Now THAT'S a poker face.*

*One of the "lean years."
"If we freeze them all in one bag,
we can pretend it's a hindquarter."*

This is a tracking snow?
Blizzard of 1985. 18.5 inches November 23.

*Don't let Myron tell you he bagged
this one after a lengthy stalk.*

The brothers two
Mike's　　　　Mert's
145#　1960　144#

Bill and Dad in "Old Bullet,"
Polk Co., WI
1974

The first deer I ever SAW!! 1955

Mert Sr. 1965
Yes, that's a '33 Ford 5 window coupe

If you can't shoot deer,
you may as well shoot pictures.

Mert, Mert Sr. Mike
Polk Co., WI
1962.

We met on an oak ridge at 10 yards.

"Let me think. Will it be Stroganoff or turkey goo for supper tonight?"

Mert and Kathy

Dad and I 1979.

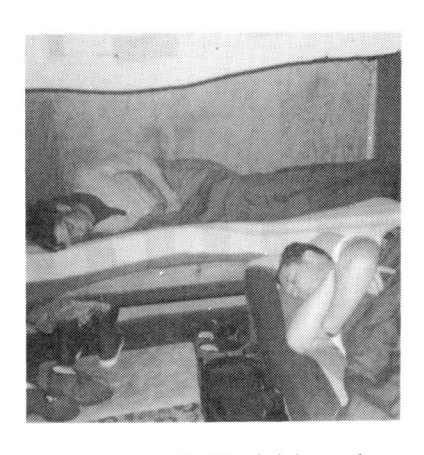

Never fear. We'll be bright-eyed, bushy-tailed, and on stand in half an hour.

"The Gruesome Foursome" with the "Campguard" Trudy.

Kirk and Dan. The results of a little friendly competition.

From the Camp Log

Fri. Nite -

Dear Log,
    Members present and accounted for:
        Barlow "Buck" Malone
        Gomer "Gut Shot" Johnson
        Calvin "Bear Breath" Calhoun
        Wilbur "Weak Eyes" Sweeny
        Bernard "Barney" Oleson
        Ralph "The Cookie" Carlson

Made poor time getting to camp again this year. Plans were to start out from home early Thurs. morning and get to camp in time to make chili, clean the shack up, and check out our stands. Buck was at the wheel of Bear Breath's '47 Plymouth sedan and was doing a fair job of keeping it between the ditches until Gut Shot unrolls the camp calendar for this year which causes Buck to take his eyes off the gravel for a second. He put us into a bog swamp, which wouldn't have been all that bad if it had been completely frozen over. We were 100 yards off the road before we dropped in. We spent last night in the car. About midnight Bear said he had to go outside so he crawled out the window and up the fender and then onto the hood. He did fine until he hit the frost on the hood and fell backwards through the windshield, right on top of Ralph and Wilbur who were trying to double bunk on the front seat. The rest of the night was chilly. We drew cattail reeds this morning to see who got to wade to the road and hike to town to get a wrecker. Ralph won. He was back with a wrecker by 10:30. Two hours, one bumper, and 100 bucks later we were back on the road.

It took 5 hours to make the last 50 miles to camp. Without the windshield, Buck complained his eyelids froze shut when he went over 10 miles an hour. We didn't need another trip into the ditch.

Camp was intact. The red squirrel that ate the window sill and made a nest out of my pillow is now hanging from the buck pole.

Gut-Shot was in such a hurry to get out of the house for 10 days he forgot the sack with his underwear on his front porch. We all dug through our extra gear to outfit him for tomorrow. Ralph was the only one with an extra set of longjohns (size 48 - Gut-Shot wears a 34-36) We cinched him up with a couple of safety pins and a couple of stitches from Ralph's handy sewing kit. One slip of the needle had four guys from the camp next door over to see what all the screaming was about. Sure feels good to be in camp again. Have to close. Big day ahead. Tomorrow's the opener.

Sat. Nite

We were all up at 4:00. Ralph took honors as cook. Gut-Shot ate breakfast twice. After Gut-Shot had started eating, Ralph told him that 3 flies had dropped onto his eggs (easy over) and to watch for them. Gut-Shot could account for only 2 at that time.

Hit for the stands at 5:45. Buck forgot to take his flashlight. Buck walked into a tree. We figure his eye should open again by Wed., or Thurs. at the latest.

At noon we met back at camp for lunch and to compare notes. Everyone had seen deer, everyone had a good excuse.

Buck said he should have had one but couldn't open his shooting eye.

Gut-Shot did just exactly that.

Ralph had a buck get past him because its ears covered up it's horns.

Weak Eyes said he saw a lot of flags but it could have been snow falling off the branches. Fortunately Weak Eyes is not a snap-shot.

I can claim I never missed a shot today. My clip fell out some where between the road and my stand.

Heavy snow this afternoon. We were all back in camp by dark. There's really something special about the smell of wet wool socks in a deer camp.

Sun. Nite

We all put in a hard day of hunting but it is almost like the deer have disappeared. Bear Breath was the only one to see a deer today. We are all concerned if this will turn into a season like we had last year, and the year before that, and...

Mon. Nite

Fresh Liver and onions for supper tonight! It was great. Weak Eyes provided us with the liver when he came across a warm gut pile this morning. Some camps frown on this practice but we figure we just saved it from the coyotes and ravens. The game wardens stopped by during supper. I figure the smell of Ralph's fried onions must have lured them in when they were driving past. They were fully prepared to fine us for an illegal deer until Weak-Eyes grabbed a flashlight and took them out to the spot where he had acquired it. They seemed satisfied and left. A friendly game of cards and we called it a night.

Tues. Nite

We all took turns sitting up last night on guard duty for two reasons. #1 the alarm clock broke and we were afraid we might oversleep #2 somebody has to get that mouse that keeps climbing up on the table and nibbles on the stick of butter. A couple of the guys are a little squeamish at the sight of tiny teeth marks. It turned out to be a waste of time however. Buck, the last man on watch, fell asleep. We woke up at 9:40 to find the mouse had done its deed to the butter. We hunted around camp today and bounced a couple of tails through the jack pines but the buck pole still stands empty. Ralph won the pot tonight with a full house, aces high. We all quit when he won and hit the bunks.

Wed Nite -

Everyone was confined to camp today. Ralph has been somewhat despondent all day. He took it personal when Weak Eyes, on his way to the outhouse, said "Anybody should know better than to leave chili out for two days and then try and serve it." By the way, we have assigned the outhouse a new nickname, "Painful Holler." We hope to be back on our feet and ready to hit it hard again tomorrow.

Thurs. Nite -

One hangs on the buck pole! Bear Breath got a dandy 6 pointer on the way to his stand this morning. He hit it when it came out of the ditch and tried to make it across the trail. That cow-catcher of a grill guard he has on that old Plymouth Sedan flipped the buck up and over the hood, across the top, and it slip down and stopped on the trunk. Bear finished it off right there.
*Note - a hole in a gas tank can temporarily be patched with a cud of fresh chewing gum. Bear also claims it helps to clear your throat when you swallow your snoose. Bear can easily patch the hole in his trunk with a piece of corrugated tin and a rivet gun come next spring. He told the guys over at a neighboring camp he got it with his 47 caliber. It was supposed to be a joke but some of them didn't know the difference. He claims this is the only way to hunt. Bear has a real hangup when it comes to long drags.

Had to scrap the card game tonight. The mouse chewed the corners off half of the cards and Ralph refuses to play with a marked deck.

Fri. Nite

We were all up early and worked the cedar

swamp west of camp. We were confident when we heard several shots coming from Barney's direction followed by a muffled finishing shot. I imagine our disappointment when Barney came out with a snowshoe rabbit, and not a very big one at that. And to think it took 5 shots for him to drop it. Bear Breath showed up about an hour late. He said he had come across a fresh blood trail which he followed through the bogs and under several deadfalls. He said he lost it down by the edge of the swamp where we were supposed to meet. I wonder why.

    Buck complained of a sore shoulder this evening. His tree stand had shifted and he hung by one arm for half an hour before he managed to pull himself back into his stand. He did have two dandy bucks pass beneath his feet, actually stepping over his rifle, as he hung there. At least its nice to know there are still some bucks around.

    We all cleaned up tonight (changed wool shirts) and headed into town tonight to the Hunter's Ball and Bouya. The plastic wrap windshield on Bear Breath's sedan proved satisfactory.

Ralph had to patch up Gut-Shot's index finger when we got back to camp. He got it stepped on during a rather wild rendition of The Bunny Hop. I haven't seen a pair of hobnailed boots like that in years, and have yet to figure why anyone would wear them to a dance. The guy couldn't even waltz. He clog stepped to every tune they played. The dance ended early when the fiddler fell off the stage and landed on his violin. We all agreed on the way back to camp that those few notes that resulted from the impact was the best music the guy had played all night.

Sat. Nite

    The gang from one of the neighboring camps paid us a visit this morning. The camp has been in the Dork family for years and is presently owned by the Dork quadruplets, Harry, Jerry, Terry, and Mary. We used to get together with them when old man Selmer was alive. Now there was a real Dork. He was one of the early pioneers in formulating and testing the use of deer lure. He was killed in a rather bizarre manner eight or ten years ago. He was bent over a scrape applying some of his new potions and never really knew what hit him, but that's another story.

The guys have never liked to hunt with the Dorks since. Weak Eyes says that it's downright embarassing to hunt with a woman that has a deeper voice than he does and can grow a better moustache than any guy in camp.

At any rate, the Dorks chose to drive first, we'd be on stand. Being quadruplets, they took off in four different directions and it was noon before we got everybody rounded up and headed back to camp. Ralph almost caused a scene when he refused to ride in the back seat with Mary. He avoided any problems by claiming he was overheated, and rode back to camp standing on the running board. As the weather was somewhat threatening, we decided to stay close to camp for the rest of the afternoon. At cards, Weak Eyes won the pot Ralph had planned to buy a new scope with, and the money Ralph was to use for camp expenses. I accepted his I.O.U.

Sun. Morn
    Woke up late. Heavy wet snow is falling (8"-10"), and the temperature is dropping. We have decided to close up camp and head for home. We have had a good season.
    We all got together again.
    We had a safe season.
    We have a storehouse full of memories.
    The camplife was great.
    We survived Ralph's cooking!

Be back next season.   Barney

When life's daily problems
    start getting you down
Or help when you need it
    is never around
If things never go
    quite according to plan
That's just what it's like
    at the "Ultimate Stand."

—Mert